# KINMEL REVISITED

## By

## Robert James Bridge

*The cover of Kinmel Revisited is of St Margaret's Church Bodelwyddan, North Wales. This is the home of five Canadian Soldiers graves, plus many more who fought bravely in each and every war!*

*"We Shall Remember Them!"*

Published by Pen It! Publications, LLC in the U.S.A.
812-371-4128  www.penitpublications.com

ISBN: 978-1-952894-36-7
Edited by Stacy Allgeier
Cover Picture Provided by Author

# Introduction

Today one could perhaps be forgiven for not noticing the small village of Bodelwyddan situated on the North Wales coast, but back in the year 1919, just after the war to end all wars, another was about to begin in the shape of a riot by some four hundred men of the Canadian expeditionary force stationed in the camp adjacent to the village, and indeed Bodelwyddan was on the front page of almost every tabloid newspaper in the country.

The year is 1990 and I, Robert Bridge, known fondly as Bob, and my wife Lilian, had decided after fifteen years working for a credit card company that it was time to maybe live near our aged parents in Abergele, another village not far from Bodelwyddan. It has to be said that because of family ties we returned South at a later date.

Meanwhile, we purchased an old Victorian house for the challenge of bringing it up to modern day standards. The house had been built around 1890 and stood in its own, ground away from the hubbub of everyday life. Our first chore was to have central heating installed, even though each and every room had an old Victorian fireplace. We then set about the many other chores that needed doing.

It came about one day, whilst Lilian was preparing

lunch, I decided it was time to clear the attic. Now the attic, like the rest of the house, had not seen the light of day for many years. As I made my way through the tangled web, I came across loads of old junk which included an old box in the corner. As I brushed away the dust, I was confronted by the insignia of a Regiment that escaped me; a regiment from many years ago. Curiosity got the better of me, so I shone my torch on the badge, brushed the dust off, and proceeded to open the box.

Lo and behold and much to my surprise, inside were a set of old manuscripts that were damp and almost unreadable. I found a crate to sit on and with the aid of my torch began to read of a story that had me mesmerized by the heading which read **"Kinmel Revisited"**.

Now, I had heard of Kinmel and the many stories that were told in the public houses and of how an army officer and his wife had lodged in Abergele in 1919 during the riot at the camp. Suddenly, it became clear as this fascinating story unfolded before me that we had, in fact, purchased the house and the manuscripts that had been written by him. Manuscripts that had remained untouched in the box all those years.

I must say, even with my torch, much of the writing had been erased, but the entire story was legible. Mesmerized by the story, I felt myself being taken aback to an era long forgotten; to trenches and men screaming out in pain, and to Kinmel camp and the riot that Captain George Sawley witnessed.

"Bob, your lunch is ready," Lilian's voice brought me back to reality.

"OK love, be down in a second," I shouted as I placed my find back in the box.

Leaving it in the attic, I went downstairs only to be confronted by Lilian. "What the hell have you been doing all this time?" she said, as I stood open mouthed.

"Lillian, you are not going to believe this but we have purchased a house in which an army officer and his wife lodged during the riot at Kinmel in 1919, and guess what, the officer wrote down the story and it's in the attic. Jesus, it isn't a treasure, but it sure makes fascinating reading!"

\*\*\*\*

That evening I brought the box down, and we tried to compile the story of the Kinmel camp riot, and of how George came to be sent to Kinmel after the war.

\*\*\*\*

The next day we took a trip over to Bodelwyddan to the churchyard of St Margaret's to see first-hand the graves of five young men, who it seems died during the fracas of bullet and bayonet wounds. I then took my find to the local historical society, and they said, although faded, it was a genuine manuscript, and maybe one day a book will tell the story of the riot at Kinmel?

We continued our chores and cleared out the attic but never came across any more papers. It seems the badge was of the Artillery, and we had the job of keeping our find in good condition until, at a later date, I decided I wanted to write a book on the Riot at Kinmel, perhaps in memory of those five young men.

# Prelude

The frantic knocking on the door awakened me from the sleep I was trying to catch up on. I stumbled to my feet, belatedly realizing that I was not still in the trenches, as the horrors of my dream seemed to indicate. The knocking continued, so I pulled open the door to be confronted by torrential rain, and a half-drowned corporal who was obviously in a state of near panic.

"Captain Sawley, Sir," he stuttered. "You must come at once! The Canadians have raided the canteen and barricade themselves in. They are well on the way to being drunk, sir, and the leader of the men is saying that if someone in authority does not tell them when they are going home, they will bring the camp to its knees. They must be armed, sir, because they are threatening to shoot anyone who comes within range if their demands aren't met."

Without waiting for a reply, the corporal saluted me and dashed off into the muck of the rain-soaked field we used as a parade ground, although it must be said that it looked more like the desolate wastes of the front than any parade ground, and sounded like it too as sporadic gunfire echoed around the camp. As I watched the man disappear into the gloom, I realized that this trouble was all mine. There was no one else to turn to but I prided myself that the Sawley name was one of honor and I, Captain George Sawley, would face this as l had faced the Germans at the front, with all the courage I could muster. It was early March and the cold winter was taking its toll. Kinmel Park Camp, sited on the outskirts of the village of Bodelwyddan in North Wales, was in the grip of a flu epidemic.

# Chapter 1

It seemed logical to me that conditions in the camp were worse than those at the front, and I almost understood why, indeed, the men rioted and for what reason. They had fought bravely for many years and watched comrades die at their feet, and all they wanted was to return home to loved ones. Of course, as an officer, I had to remain independent and not take sides since it was British buildings etc. that were being destroyed, but may I take you on a journey back in time to a world that had seen thousands of young men die for no apparent reason?

It was 1919 and the camp was built to house some 29,000 men of various nationalities; the bulk of the men were Canadians, men who had fought bravely during a war that never seemed to end; where so many brave men died for no apparent reason. A war that lasted for five long years when mere boys became men as they dashed headlong into carnage seeing men they had befriended dying or dead in the mud of the battle. Men who, when the war eventually ended, only wanted to go back to their homeland, but there were no ships for transport. So, they were sent to Kinmel to kick their heels and await transport, creating a ferment of discontent and anger.

On Tuesday March the fourth 1919, it finally happened and men who had been driven almost to a frenzy by a small group of russo-bolshovics rioted; some called it a mutiny, others a riot, but whatever the true term was it made no difference. The camp quickly came under the control of the rioters; at a later date it was said that only some 400 men were involved, but it seemed to me that there were far more as the camp deteriorated into yet another war zone, if anything far worse than the one I had so recently left behind, because these men had been comrades in arms against a common enemy.

After the attack on the canteen, it seemed inevitable that the next to suffer would be the liquor store and close behind a raid on the local shops known as Tintown because of their metal construction.

Eventually the rioters attacked the village of Abergele, then onward to the township of Rhyl. British troops were ordered to attempt to restore order, but it was a difficult task, because all the men wanted to do was go home and although the British had to obey orders, they were in sympathy with the Canadians because of their unfair treatment, yet at the same time the British could not excuse the wanton killings.

As an officer, I knew it was my duty to attempt to restore order and although these men and I had fought side by side in the past. My duty was clear, and I knew that I would carry out my commitments, but it was with bleak and aching heart that I stood almost waist deep in the mud and rain.

The camp was besieged with unrest long before I myself arrived, mainly because the men were finding life boring after so much activity. The feeling was also rife among the British contingent, although they were used to unholy conditions in the trenches, they had little or no entertainment and became unpopular with the locals because of their drunken binges in the towns, many times hordes of men would return from a drinking session and head for the wet canteen as it was known, to resume drinking and inevitably fighting would break out between the British and Canadian soldiers.

****

The daily existence for the shifting population of some 20,000 men waiting for passage was cold, damp, and most of all monotonous. The seventy-five military policemen whose job it was to guard the camp had rifles but no ammunition, their only means of defense were bayonets which remained in their scabbards, they also complained that they got no extra pay for guarding men who, like themselves, wanted to go home.

The flu epidemic was taking its toll, and this added to the unrest which was almost at boiling point. I had found lodgings in the small town of Abergele that were large enough to accommodate myself and my wife, Mildred. So, unlike many of my fellow officers, I was able to return to my lodgings after my days in the camp.

\*\*\*\*

I remember clearly the day Mildred and myself arrived at Rhyl railway station to be met by a burly sergeant with a large moustache; as he sprang to attention, it was clear he had seen many years of service and his Scottish accent became evident as he said, "Sergeant Charles Mclaren, Kings own Scottish at your service, sir." He pointed to the waiting motor car as I said, "I thought Major Underwood was meeting us, Sergeant?" "Er, yes sir, the major sends his apologies, bit of trouble at the camp, sir."

Mildred and I found, although the scenery was magnificent, the roads were very bumpy.

"Very cold here sir, especially this time of year, reminds me of my hometown of Glasgow. I see, sir, you have seen a lot of action?" the sergeant said.

"How come you know that sergeant?" I replied.

"Well sir, begging your pardon, but when the motor car backfired you almost jumped out of your skin and only someone who had been in the trenches would have reacted so. I too did my bit for King and country sir, so I reckon I know a seasoned officer when I see one."

As the car headed in the direction of Abergele, I knew instinctively from rumors I would be met with disobedience and general unrest."

"Why are those men not on their way home,

Sergeant?" I asked.

"Well, sir it seems the ships are being used for commercial purposes and the owners want them back. Plus, rumor has it the yanks have been given priority, sir."

As we approached Abergele and our lodgings, I wondered what the future held.

Mrs. Jones was the lady we would be staying with. She was a kindly lady who was ready to disclose the drunken fights she had witnessed in the town. After giving us a tour of the house and discussing mealtimes and other itinerary, I decided I should report to the camp and see firsthand what, in fact, was wrong. At first sight, all seemed normal, that is until it became evident there was a distinct lack of discipline. The men were untidy and many had cigarettes hanging from their mouths, jackets undone and were refusing to return my salute.

The camp was under the command of Colonel Rufus J. Brown, an experienced officer who had lost a leg in the war. He was known as a lenient man who had a lot of sympathy for the Canadians. He was, in fact, at the War Office in London upon my arrival. So, I was introduced to Major John Underwood who was standing in for him.

"Er, George Sawley, I believe? Sorry I was unable to meet you, old chap, but the Canadians are getting restless."

John Underwood, an ex-Eton boy, had never seen service at the front and had been given his rank after attending Sandhurst. Daddy, it seems, was a well-known barrister in the City.

As he opened his mouth to speak, another fight broke out. "Sorry, old boy, got to sort this out, will speak later.'"

As I decided it was time I returned to Abergele, a young corporal ran by and I stopped him: "What is going on, corporal?" I inquired.

"Seems a colored guy had broken a M.P.s jaw. They released the Canadian guy and it seems like the camp is about to explode Sir!'"

****

Mildred was aware of the unrest in the camp and feared for my safety, but as I explained it was my job and I had seen far worse at the front, she seemed to calm down a little. As I began my first week at Kinmel camp, it became clear that if the ships did not become available soon, the camp would erupt into what can only be described as a blood begrimed sea of bodies.

Although, Tuesday, March 4, 1919, was the day the rioters took command of the camp; previous to that, on March 1st, whilst having tea, I was informed some three hundred men were about to raid the canteen, and since this had women working inside, many of those in charge were very concerned. It seemed the men had intentions to ransack the canteen and remove the goods. The fear was for the women and the shops locally (at the court martial it was mentioned that some of the women were in fact raped, but this was never proven and not one woman came forward).

That evening the camp went very quiet. Maybe the men had got what they wanted or were too drunk to cause any more trouble, but for the next few days, it was seeming as though it was all over, that is until the morning I was awoken by the frantic knocking and the corporal standing in the rain; the morning of March 4th 1919. I had confronted the might of the German army, but knowing the Canadians outnumbered the British, I felt for once my life was in danger. I began to think of Mildred and the other civilians in the township, and as I kissed Mildred goodbye, I warned her to be especially vigilant. I was thinking to myself as I approached the camp, I would sooner face the wrath of the German army than face the men I had every sympathy for.

The scene that confronted me was of complete disarray; groups of men were smashing everything in sight. Drunken hordes were ordered to return to their quarters as they began shouting obscenities such as, "This is the thanks we get for fighting a bloody war for them?" As the speaker stopped, it was noticeable he was drinking from a bottle which he proceeded to smash on the ground.

The order came through to remove my pistol but not to load it since the idea was to threaten the men without too much bloodshed. Waving my pistol around, I felt a complete fool, but it did have the desired effect in some areas. During my short time in the trenches I had experienced the sight of men dying and screaming out in pain as they waited for death to show its ugly face. So, I was no stranger to violence. Suddenly I felt a crushing blow and began to feel the warm flow of blood running down my face. As darkness descended upon me, I heard a voice shout," It's Captain Sawley. The bastards have smashed his bloody head in?"

# Chapter 2

**I** don't remember what happened next. All I knew was the smell of cordite was evident and the shelling began once more. I saw myself crouched in the trench shaking with fear, all around me men were screaming in pain. The trench was half full of cold wet mud since the rain never seemed to stop. Night after night, I would pray for the shelling to stop as the screams seemed endless; screams that would remain in my head until the day I died.

Many times since returning home Mildred cradled me in her arms like a baby as night after night I would wake up shouting for the men to go over the top, sweating so profusely cold towels had to be administered. Slowly opening my eyes, I realized I must have been screaming out again, but this time it was not Mildred holding me, it was a nurse who smelt of starch. My head felt ready to explode as I instinctively reached up to feel the bandages, the shelling began once more and I found myself issuing orders above the screams of men in pain.

"Now there, sir, you have had a nasty bang on the head and it's brought back many bad memories."

Although I had lost a lot of blood, I tried in vain to sit up, and as I fell back onto the pillow I was blinded by the light on the ceiling, a light that only reminded me of the shelling that never ceased.

The vision as my head began to clear was one of white walls and the smell of clean linen; it was then I realized I was not in the trench but in the safety of the Hospital. The room slowly came into focus, and I realized there were two people standing by the bed. One of them had taken my hand, and I knew it was Mildred.

"George it's me, Mildred; you sure took a nasty blow."

The other person in a white coat also came into view and said, "Steady, old boy, you are not strong enough to sit up yet. By the way I am your doctor Major John Lepage, and before you ask, I am not American but Canadian." He then turned to Mildred and said, "Well, there is no loss of memory, just memories that will eventually go. He needs plenty of rest, and I am sure with your help it won't be too long before he is back on his feet."

As he turned and left the room, Mildred said, "Looks like you don't need me, George. You are in capable hands."

"How long have I…" I started to say.

Mildred replied, "How long have you been unconscious you are about to ask? Well, it's been almost two days since you were hit over the head, and to tell the truth, we were getting concerned for your memory because for two days, you have been reliving your time in the trenches."

"The camp," I started to say as once more Mildred interrupted.

"The camp is in turmoil and rumor has it that some have died during the riot. They have arrested the man who hit you over the head, so please George leave it to those who are capable of dealing with it."

As Mildred stood up to leave, she continued, "I will be in to see you tomorrow my love, just get some rest." As she turned to leave, her words echoed in my ears, "Let them who are capable deal with it." I felt the onus was on me to deal with it; the guilt hung heavily on my shoulders because, as an officer, I was a leader of men, and it was my duty to try and restore order.

It would seem I had been given a sedative since I began once again to slip back into my worst nightmare. One by one faces of friends I had known came back to me. The rain sodden trench began to fill with water as I placed my whistle to my mouth ordering the men to go over the top, seeing myself scrambling in the sea of mud to try and reach the top of the trench, only to be fought back by men who had blood running down their faces, and men who were minus arms or legs. "God help us," I said to the corporal sitting next to me, only to realize he had received a bullet to the head and was dead.

****

Once more, I placed the whistle to my mouth and began to pull myself through the mud. As I reach the top, a flash of light hit me full in the face as another shell landed, and the screaming resumed, screaming that I found I was unable to forget.

"Now there, sir, you have had another of those dreams?" Her soft voice seemed a million miles away until my eyes cleared and she came into view; she had short boyish hair with a tiny white hat perched on top of it, and she had a smile I am sure would melt the hearts of many a soldier.

"Could I have some tablets please, nurse? My head is about to explode."

Her Welsh accent was clear as she replied, "Here you are, sir. Take these and lay back, you probably have a temperature. By the way, sir, my name is Ellie, Ellie Jones, and I am to be your nurse until you get better." As she proceeded to give me the tablets, she said, "Must have been terrible, sir. The last two days you have been to hell and back. I lost my father in the war, sir, Sergeant David Jones or Davy as he was known, shell landed in the trench, it did, sir," Ellie said with a lump in her throat.

"Sorry to hear that Ellie."

Each day Ellie would tell me what was going on at the camp, and it soon became clear some of the men had been killed during the riot. One of them was the trooper who had hit me over the head. Apparently he had been killed by a bayonet to the stomach, a terrible way to die for a man who only wanted to go home.

His name was Ivan Velitch, age thirty, and he was of Russian parents; the precise way he died never became clear as was the case of many of those who died during that terrible time.

Punctuated by death, the fighting began once more in earnest, and it was not too long before the second death was recorded. This one was to die in the ward next to my own. Corporal Jimmy Smith, age thirty-six, had been hacked in the face by a bayonet and had died of his wounds. It would seem he had only been in the camp some twenty-four hours after returning from the front, an innocent bystander it seems, who was killed just for being in the wrong place at the wrong time.

News of the riot soon spread and it was not long before the Liverpool Echo was awash with news of the deaths. Kinmel camp, largely unknown until that time, was now on the front page of every tabloid from Lands' End to Scotland. Nurse Ellie told me the riot at the camp was escalating, and ignore it. Though I tried, even though my sympathies lay with the men, I felt it my duty to return to the camp against doctors' orders and of course Mildred's. Ellie begged me to stay since she said I was still unwell; but duty was duty and even though my head was about to explode, I discharged myself and returned to what was left of the camp.

Mildred's wrath was worse than I imagined as she said, "My God, even though your head is about to explode your loyalty still remains steadfast to the army?"

With my hat perched precociously on my bandaged head, I replied, "With a head like mine, who wants to get involved in the fracas?"

Mildred was aware that I could sometimes be stubborn and the second most important thing in my life was the army. So, she didn't pursue the argument any further.

I was not prepared for the sight that confronted me as I approached the camp. Tintown (the local shops) had been raised to the ground, and the impounding area was littered with empty beer bottles. Rioters were shouting obscenities at the officers. As I joined my fellow officers, I realized they had drawn their pistols and were about to fire over the heads of the flag waving men. Suddenly, about twenty or thirty men began to advance towards us.

My friend of long-standing Lt John Wylie shouted, "Look out George, that fellow is about to give you another head wound."

The plank of wood missed me by inches. In an attempt to frighten the man, I fired my pistol over his head as he collapsed in a drunken heap singing to himself as he did.

As I replaced my pistol, I wondered how many were in fact involved in the riot, since it seemed to me many were so drunk they were caught up in something they did not understand. As the day progressed and the riot got more intense, the third fatality became apparent and this the one that made me feel sick because of his young age, sick because at nineteen years old his young life had been cut short.

Private John Henry was shot in the back of the head holding off the rioters' advance, as he fell to the ground, I cradled his young head in my arms and tried to stop the flow of blood. Realizing he was dead, I removed my jacket and placed it over his body as the fighting resumed. I had seen many men die, but the sight of that young man made me feel violently sick. At the time, I did not know his name, so I looked in his bloodstained jacket and came across what I knew was his mother and father.

With his head still in my arms, I wept and began to shout, "How are you going to explain to this boy's parents that their son was shot in the head doing his duty?"

Suddenly the fighting stopped and an uncanny silence made its eerie way through the camp. I reached down with tears running down my face and picked up his limp body. Suddenly a passage opened between the rioters and I could feel the disbelief as I carried him towards the open door of one of the huts. Silence remained as my tears mingled with his blood. As I got to the door, I turned and shouted, "I hope you are all satisfied now! This is one young man who will never see his family again."

I suppose one should not grieve for every death one comes across, but that day left a mental scar on my mind that will remain with me forever. Although I never knew Private Henry, I grieved not only for him but also his family who were left to wonder why their son had died such a death in a camp somewhere in Wales. Many years after I would stand at his grave and weep uncontrollably.

# Chapter 3

What were thought to be the ringleaders were dispatched to Liverpool jail to await the court of inquiry and the subsequent trials, whilst the remainder was placed under close arrest. It emerged that, in total, five men had died during the riot and twenty-eight were injured. With the ringleaders out of the way, we hoped things would return to normal, but we were wrong because, rumor had it, some of those not locked up were talking of revenge in the shape of the shops in the town of Rhyl. I prayed this was not true since more deaths, I feared, would only re-light the fuse, as it were.

That same evening after returning home I was met by Mildred who had heard of the young man's death and explained how the residents of Abergele and surrounding areas were worried the situation might spread.

In an attempt to calm the situation down, the War Office, in its wisdom, decided to send a war hero down to Kinmel to explain why the ships were still not available. A hero in that he had committed many deeds beyond the call of duty, none less than carrying a wounded man on his shoulders through the darkness of enemy lines, back to the safety of his regiment, a heroic deed that was recognized by awarding him the Victoria Cross, possibly the highest honor a soldier could receive from his country.

The morning of the sixth of March 1919 was cold, wet and very windy. As I sat eating my breakfast, the anticipation that I was to meet a real war hero was making me nervous, and it showed, because Mildred said, "For God's sake George, he is only human like the rest of us. I am sure you would have done exactly has he did."

"I don't know Mildred, who knows what we would do given the same situation?"

"Lieutenant General George Smithers V.C. was a tall imposing man with a large moustache and a uniform dripping with medals. As he stepped from the motor car, I saluted him and held out my hand in a friendly gesture. Colonel Brown had returned from the War Office, and I introduced him to the General who immediately led him towards the officers' quarters. An eerie silence once again came over the camp, and the rioters, as they stood almost in awe of this man; a man who one knew would not be intimidated by any man living. A man who feared nothing, since he had come face to face with death on many occasions.

That day, Lt General George Smithers V. C. addressed some fifteen meetings stating the S.S. Celtic was ready to depart on the tenth of March for Canada and most men would be on it. Also a two-pound advance would be given to each and every man. He even mentioned a possible amnesty for those who looted the stores, but since five men had died, those in jail would be held responsible for inciting not only a riot, but for the deaths of those men.

"The trials of the men in jail are, of course, out of my hands, but I can promise each man will be given a fair hearing. At this juncture, I am unable to comment further until the result of the inquiry is known."

The men were overjoyed at the prospect of returning home and a few extra shillings. Some complained of the mates who were left in jail, but no mention was made of the five dead men. The General was given a rousing cheer as he left each meeting, whilst I myself was a little apprehensive as to who would be the first to board the S.S. Celtic. I also wondered why for some reason the five deaths were not mentioned, or in fact, who killed them.

A great many of the tabloids were running riot with rumors, most of which were unfounded. One paper stated and I quote, "Some 6,000 soldiers, mainly Canadian, were on the rampage at Kinmel Park army camp in North Wales and some of the local civilians i.e. women had been molested during the fracas." One paper even went as far to mention rape, and this did nothing to silence the men and their anger. It was decided it was time to issue a statement to clarify the truth.

"Five men died as a result of some unrest at Kinmel camp, twenty-one received wounds, and the ammunition used during the riot had been brought back from the war." Since a case was still missing, we knew this to be untrue. The men under close arrest were given the task of cleaning up the debris and this, of course, caused them to be disgruntled.

Whilst this was going on, I approached the medical hut and it resembled a first aid trench at the front. Many of the men were in bandages and some were on crutches. My next port of call was the hut containing the row of five coffins neatly draped with the ensign of the maple leaf. It was not until I reached Private John Henry's coffin that I felt the emotion building up inside of me, and as I placed my hand on the flag that was draped over it, I felt I must say my last goodbyes. "God be with you son, you did not deserve such a death; someday, some time they will remember you."

\*\*\*\*

The inquest on the five dead men was, to all intents, an open and shut case since they were unable to find who or how they got killed. Since this was March 7th, and those who had been allocated berths on the S.S. Celtic were packing, ready to leave for Liverpool.

Saturday the 8th of March was designated as the day the five would be buried in the churchyard of St Margaret's Church, known fondly as the Marble Church because of its marble exterior. It was decided because of the burials the whole proceedings would be moved to Liverpool, and that the trial of those in jail would continue along with finalization of the said inquest.

So without further ado, the inquest was adjourned for one week to gather more evidence the inquiry stated, and since this was an army matter and not a civilian one, an embargo would be put on all press coverage. Of course this did little to stem the flow of rumors which gradually spread around the towns and surrounding areas, rumors that Mildred as an officer's wife heard daily from the locals. Since it emerged the women who worked in the canteen at the camp had been told to get a checkup at their doctors, many said it was because they were abused and some even said they had been raped during the riot, but nothing was further from the truth since each and every civilian worker was removed under escort almost as soon as the riot began.

# Chapter 4

On the morning of Saturday 8th March 1919, an eerie peace seemed to descend on the town of Abergele and the surrounding area. Horse drawn carriages were to take the men to their last resting place along with their comrades who had fought bravely with them; my thoughts went out not only to their families but to those who had killed them since they now had to endure the prospect of seeing their friends buried in St Margaret's along with many other servicemen from various nationalities.

Although only a short journey to the church I could see many of the British, as well as Canadian soldiers, were almost in tears and as the procession entered the churchyard, I felt a cold wind blowing over the hills and mountains. One by one each coffin was lowered into its last resting place, and the silence was only broken by the sound of the bugler as he began to play the last post and the vicar as he prayed for each of them to rest in peace.

As the rain began, Mildred and I pledged to return each year to place a flower on each and every grave; even though we hardly knew those men we felt it our duty to pay our respects and thanks for keeping our country free from the invading enemy.

## The Trials!

The trials of those involved were to begin in earnest on 16th April 1919. Fifty-one men were to be tried and court martialed for their part in the Kinmel camp riot, and even though the man who hit me over the head was now dead, it seems because I was injured and the mere fact that I was involved in the riot, plus since they said I had witnessed most of it; I was ordered to attend the trials much to my annoyance and total disbelief.

Ruska Romonoff lived with her mother and father in poverty in Moscow unaware her twin brother Frederick had been arrested for striking an officer and was in jail. Frederick had left home to make his fortune in Canada, but upon arrival he could not get employment. So, he joined the Canadian forestry corps. Frederick served with distinction and for his heroism had been awarded the medal of honor, an award no other Russian had ever received. His family was proud of him until the War Office informed them of his misdeed during the riot. Ruska tried to console her parents who said he had brought shame on the family. Frederick knew he had done wrong, but his English was so poor he failed to understand what was going on. Meanwhile Ruska attempted to prove his innocence by saying the war had affected him mentally and he should not be blamed for an act of violence that was not entirely his own making.

Ruska was to be a big influence on the trials. Her parents had given her all their savings just so she could come to England and attend the trial of her brother. Since I knew the trials would take some time, I decided to return home to Abergele daily, and at the end of the first day which consisted of reading out each and every one of the men and their offences, I was met at Rhyl railway station by Mildred who led me towards what can only be described as a four wheel monster. It had an open top, which I figured in rain-swept Wales, was not a good idea. I stood open mouthed as Mildred climbed behind the driving seat with an impish smile on her face.

"Just think George, no more taxis and the open road before us."

I sat in amazement unable to speak as the rain once more started; as Mildred stopped, I reached for the canopy to pull over but it came as no surprise when I found it had a large hole in it. Unperturbed, I climbed back in and said, "The wind, rain and the open road eh?"

Mildred replied, "Don't be an old spoilsport, George. Think of it as an adventure."

Suddenly the car backfired as Mildred said or rather shouted, "How did the first day go, George?"

To avoid the wind and rain I pulled up my collar and replied, "I will tell you if we ever get to Abergele."

After supper I sat warming myself by the coal fire and reflected on one of the men accused, a young private by the name of Jack Haines; a Canadian lad who had fought bravely in the battle for Vimy Ridge. He was born on 21st Sept 1902 and had enlisted in May 1916. Only fourteen, he had lied about his age since he wanted to become a soldier just like his ancestors. He was soon found out and discharged, only to re-enlist at a later date and become a poison gas veteran. Most of his involvement in the riot was put down to boyish enthusiasm because of his youth, the young man from the 42 Battalion Royal Highlanders of Canada had a broad smile on his face the day he was sentenced, just one of many whose only real crime was to want to go home.

As the scotch I had been drinking took its desired effect, the face of a lone soldier seemed to appear in the flames of the fire, a face that was to return to me night after night. The face of Private Henry would, I fear, haunt me for the rest of my life.

Private Jack Haines you might be thinking was just another of those protesting about the failure to get them home, and in some ways you might be right, but his story was somewhat different from the others since he was the youngest, and at fourteen he had seen more than any other boy of his age. As he sat in the cold trench shaking, not only from the cold, but in fear as the bodies all around him mounted up, he began sobbing and this soon attracted one of his superiors. When the whistle went, Jack would remain in the trench sobbing; after being branded a coward he was sent back to his own lines where it was discovered he had lied about his age. The determination and guts of this young man should not go unrecognized because three years later Jack was waiting with his birth certificate along with a letter from his father stating Jack was of age. This time Jack knew what to expect, but nevertheless, he went on to fight with devotion and courage beyond reproach, to be sent to an army camp in the middle of nowhere was far worse than the trench he had recently vacated. Jack had only been at the camp two days when, a victim of circumstances, he got caught up in the riot. Urged on by a gang of thugs, Jack felt he had to stand by his mates. At his trial, he looked almost like a schoolboy as he stood amongst men a lot older than himself.

# Chapter 5

The trials were to be continued the following Monday, so on the Saturday I returned to the camp since a rumor was going around that those awaiting shipment home had been drinking in the town of Rhyl and trouble was imminent. Trouble in the form of a New York tailor by the name of Rick Bradley, a loud-mouthed individual who had been arrested by the Provost Sergeant Gilbert Smith. Bradley, it seems, was bragging in a cafe in Rhyl about how he had molested the women at the camp, of how after raping one of them the others got excited. This, of course, was complete fabrication, but in the cafe was a Lt. Sheldon, and he had overheard Bradley ranting. Since he was a perfectionist and an army man, Sheldon made a written record of Bradley's every word and also the names Bradley had mentioned assisted him during the so-called rape.

Lt. Sheldon, because of his manner, became unpopular with many of the Canadian soldiers. I myself could not wait to hear Sheldon's evidence at the continuation of the trials. Up until now, I never mentioned my father since, as an only son and his liking for work, we never really got on. Because of my mother suddenly taken ill, I felt it my duty to go down to Cornwall and pay my respects. Since I had to return on Monday, the only day free was Sunday. So, even though I did not like Mildred's motor car, I asked her to take me.

James Sawley, my father, was in fact a prominent criminal lawyer who spent most of his time in London, and as a young man, I myself hardly knew him. It was obvious he found it a chore leaving London when my mother became ill, but since she was in fact dying of cancer, he felt it his duty to attend. Mother was very frail as Mildred and I held her hands, her voice was croaky as she tried to ask about Kinmel.

"Don't you go worrying about the camp mama," I said as I stood up. "Just going to have a word with..." I started to say.

"George don't you go arguing with him," Mildred said.

My father was lighting his pipe as I strolled out on the patio. I wondered if he would show any feeling, but I was wrong as he said, "Old girl's not got long to go."

I thought to myself, you bloody selfish old man as I said, "For once can we act like a family and not argue?"

He turned and replied, "Damn business at that camp hey? I hear you got a bang on your head. Did they ever find out who killed those five young men?" he asked.

"No, and I doubt whether they ever will," I

replied.

"Of course, as a criminal civilian lawyer I am not allowed to get involved, but they can waive their rights to an army lawyer if they so wish," he said, as he lit his pipe once more.

Now my father was a terrible husband and an even worse father, but as a lawyer there was no-one to touch him. His reputation went before him. He was well known for defensive bargaining power, but since this was an army matter, I thanked him and said I would let him know if any of the men decided they wanted a civilian to act for them.

The doctor said he would contact us if there was any change, and mother insisted I return for the trial. I don't know why but father held out his hand for me to shake and kissed Mildred goodbye. He too had to return to London since he was in court on the Monday. I don't know why, but I suddenly felt this was the last time I would see my mother.

＊＊＊＊

For no apparent reason, the proceedings were moved to London, much to my disapproval. I was told to attend, and although Mildred objected, she too came with me after contacting my mother's doctor in Cornwall. To this day I fail to understand why it was moved, but all the paperwork and witnesses had to be transferred to London. Mildred gave a cough as the carriage taking us to London filled with smoke.

I leaned towards the open window and began to close it - we had both taken window seats in the hopes the air would keep us awake on the long journey. As the steam train made its familiar noise on the tracks, I glanced out of the window only to be once more confronted by Private John Henry pleading with me to help him. As he vanished, a picture of his coffin appeared and was being lowered into the grave. As it went lower and lower, it began to rain - rain I never felt because it was in fact on the window outside.

As I came back to reality, Mildred said, "Looks like more rain, George."

Chelsea barracks were to be the venue for the proceedings, and although we were offered quarters in the barracks, Mildred and I decided it might be a better option to stay in one of the nearby hotels. Little did we realize our stay was to be cut short, and that final sentencing was to take place in Grace Road Barracks, Liverpool on the 16th April 1919. Why, we never understood, since this was only going to be a burden on the taxpayers of England, but as an officer is was my duty to not argue and obey my orders.

Under guard, I was eventually allowed to meet and talk to many of the men whom I knew not only in Kinmel, but also on the battlefield. It soon became clear to me that the riot could have been avoided along with the deaths had we been able to supply the ships to take our allies home, and although fifty-one were in jail only a handful were responsible for inciting the others to riot.

At a later date, having met each of the men, I came to the conclusion they were badly represented, and wondered, indeed, where the words innocent until proven guilty came from? Yes of course they were guilty of inciting a riot and destroying government property, but I also felt we were to blame for not getting them home? As each man came to attention in front of his superiors, I felt defending council had little or no time for them.

It was then I was informed that my mother had passed away, and I was to attend her funeral in Cornwall immediately.

# Chapter 6

The small village of Bodelwyddan was beginning to enjoy notoriety it had never known before as the worlds press got hold of the story of the Riot and the deaths. The lodging houses and the public houses were enjoying the visitors that arrived daily, some to interview the locals and some just to see the graves. The only problem was the story of the riot changed daily, like the weather, and all sorts of stories suddenly appeared in the papers. Upon our return to Abergele, we found the town buzzing with rumors.

The trials were going badly and the men were feeling they would be given harsh sentences, even though many were only in attendance during the fracas. The tall Russian Ivor Romonoff was one of the first to say he was not getting a fair trial. His outburst only gave the officers reason to believe he was one of those who whipped the men into frenzy, a leader who the panel felt would object to almost everything.

The trials were becoming more and more of a fiasco as it became clear Lt. Sheldon had attempted to bribe a prisoner by offering him a lighter sentence if he gave him the names of those who incited the men to riot, also many of the witnesses had already gone home on the S.S. Celtic. The bribery account was never proven, but the prisoner swore on oath Lt. Sheldon wanted revenge and this was his way of getting it. Sheldon, a man unpopular with the men, refused to admit his guilt, even though he himself was a Canadian. At a later date, retribution for the lies he had told was to come to him in the form of a thrashing.

Captain John Smithers of the Royal Regiment of Wales, a leading lawyer who had in the past defended men who felt wrongly accused, was to become defense lawyer for the men. Lt. Smithers, a young man still only in his twenties, had not seen action since he spent most of his time studying for the bar. Many said he was weak and they had little confidence in him, but I knew him to be an honorable man who I felt would see the men got a fair trial. Many times he would approach me on how the riot came about and of how the deaths came about: of course, I could only tell him what I saw and how I got hit over the head. Lt. Smithers felt insecure since he was not at the camp but I assured him I would give him my side of events before he met each man.

With time against him, Lt. Smithers felt he would lose, but not before he had given each and every one of them a fair hearing, and indeed on 6th June 1919 at the final hearings, seventeen of the men were acquitted. Unfortunately, twenty-four of those remaining were found guilty of various charges ranging from mutiny to assaulting an officer and destroying army property which ran into thousands of pounds, also resisting arrest. There was no mention of the civilian workers or of the so-called rape, nor were the deaths of the five men even mentioned. I myself found this to be very strange since those who were involved in the killing of the men seemed to be absolved from any responsibility.

The doctor who attended the wounded was called to give his evidence, and the ruling was the wounds they received were a direct result of drunken behavior and none were inflicted intentionally

Smithers was sitting next to me. He jumped to his feet and said, "I would, if I may Sirs, like to mention the death of Private John Henry, a young man still only nineteen was shot in the back of the head as he was advancing towards his fellow countrymen in an effort to hold them back, would the court be good enough to explain how this was possible, and how he was shot by the rioters?"

A hush descended over the proceedings as the trial officers began talking to each other.

Colonel Richmond, a seasoned officer of many years began, by saying, "Lt. Smithers, to reiterate the enquiry into those that were killed during the Kinmel camp riot has been completed and is of no relevance to this trial since it was impossible to define who the guilty party or parties were."

As Lt Smithers sat down, he whispered to me, "This trial is a bloody farce, those five men died for nothing and will never be vindicated."

The final total amount of damages to army

property came to a staggering seventy thousand pounds, and would of course, never be recuperated, but again, I thought the blame lay heavily on the government for not supplying more blankets and fuel to help the men through a winter of discontent.

Bribery was now on the agenda since many wanted to be on the first ship home, but once again, this was never proven. The presiding officers, in their wisdom, decided the damage to property and the general lack of discipline, plus inciting a riot of some proportion was enough to warrant prison sentences and indeed sentencing would begin the following day.

As the men were herded away, it was clear they felt let down since they uttered words like, "This is the thanks we get," and "unfair trial." One man even yelled out "What about those poor devils in the graveyard?"

That evening, along with Lt Smithers, I was able to meet each and every man, and as I sat listening to their grievances, I felt maybe if things had been different these men would be at home now with their loved ones. Each man thanked Lt. Smithers for his help and said they were sorry for what they had done.

After the meetings, I spoke to Lt. Smithers and he agreed this was a terrible tragedy that could have been avoided. He also agreed that the next day the men were going to receive harsh sentences and would, in fact, still not be going home for a very long time.

****

Upon my return home to Abergele that evening, Mildred told me to pour myself a large scotch since she had some news for me; news I thought would never be a possibility. Mildred informed me I was to become a father, to which I poured another large scotch and said, "I never dreamed it possible, my love."

I made a point of not mentioning how the trials were going because Mildred had met many of the accused on her shopping expeditions, she often remarked how polite they were and how she thought the shopkeepers were charging the men more than the locals because of the back pay they were receiving.

# Chapter 7

The soldiers remaining in the camp were being shipped home as fast as the ships became available, but this did nothing to stop the locals fearing another outbreak and many were still afraid to venture out of their homes. I myself had worked alongside Lt Smithers so it was possible for me to see the dossiers on most of the men and one such man was Private Jan Roskovitch, a Polish immigrant who had only been in Canada a few months but in that time had picked up enough of the language to help him get by. Jan had been warned not to leave Poland by his family but since unemployment was rampant and many families were poverty-stricken Canada, it seemed, held a better future for him. A large man, almost six-foot-tall and broadly built, Jan had cropped hair and a tattoo on each arm, tattoos of his sister Krista and of Anna, a girl he once knew. Jan had enlisted mainly because of the pay and a chance to fight for a cause, plus the uniform which attracted many of the girls. He was to all intents a loner, but it became clear if upset he would cause great damage.

Jan had fought bravely in France and was known to be a leader of men. Since he had not really a command of the English language, he could not understand why he had been sent to Kinmel camp, he only knew he had to obey orders. Jan was feared because of his size but deep down he had a pleasant nature, in fact it was he that hit one of his comrades for killing a mouse that had entered the barracks. Jan had a lack of understanding so this made him a prime target for work many of the others got away with, work that consisted of cookhouse duties and work cleaning out the latrines. For a man such as Jan, this was degrading, but he simply never knew how to say no. Jan Roskovitch was, in fact, like many others a victim of circumstances.

The weather in Warsaw was somewhat colder than that of North Wales. Krista Roskovitch, Jan's sister, was still only twenty, but looked more like fifty, as she stooped to pick up a potato that had fallen from a lorry. As she stuffed the potato in her apron, she was unable to feel her fingers because of the cold. She then made her way to the room she had above Mr. Spiegal's tailor shop; he himself was an old man in his sixties who had allowed Krista to live there since he was an old family friend. Krista had read in the papers the war in Europe had ended and began to wonder if her Brother Jan would return home to Poland or Canada.

Mr. Spiegel looked over the perched glasses he had on the end of his nose and said, "Have you seen the papers today, Krista?"

"No, I have not Mr. Spiegal, my hands are so cold I don't think I could hold the paper."

"Looks like many of the Canadian soldiers have been sent to a camp in Wales, no ships to bring them home they say, some kind of riot by the men at the camp it says, let's hope your Jan has kept out of it."

Krista climbed the cold staircase praying her brother Jan was not involved in the Riot at Kinmel. Jan Roskovitch was in fact amongst those still remaining in Kinmel camp, no reason was given, save for the fact he hardly spoke English and because of his size many thought him to be backward, but since the riot Jan was like an unexploded bomb, ready to explode at any given minute. As he cleaned the latrines, it seems some of those going home began to ridicule him and this tipped him over the edge. Approaching the mess hall, he picked up a six-foot table and hurled it in a fit of rage across the room: luckily the mess hall was empty or many would have been wounded. Suddenly all hell broke loose and we knew we were about to live our worst nightmare. Rumor had it that Jan had found a rifle and a box of ammunition and was about to hold the camp to ransom. This was a man who hardly spoke English, unable to understand why he along with the others was not on his way home, loose in the camp with a loaded rifle and enough rage inside to bring the camp to its knees. Fear spread throughout the camp as Jan talked of taking hostages and all this simply because he could not be left alone.

I myself understood perhaps why Jan had exploded. As an officer, it was my duty to apprehend him and possibly place him under close arrest, but this was not going to be an easy task since it became clear

Jan had now taken a hostage, and it was none other than the most unpopular officer in Kinmel camp, Lt. Sheldon, a man whom many still believed was guilty of bribery. After pleading with Jan to let him go, Sheldon found he was not getting through to the man because Jan never understood what he was saying. Jan had stood Sheldon on one of the tables and placed a rope around his neck knowing if the table collapsed Sheldon would hang, or if he tried to jump, he would also hang. Many of us outside knew if Sheldon's legs got tired, he would fall and hang himself. Even though he was not liked by many of us, we felt the poor man would be shaking in fear.

I turned to one of my fellow officers and said, "Let's hope he does not shake the table too much."

Finger resting precariously on the trigger, Jan was not the fool many had thought him, he knew he would possibly hang himself if he killed Sheldon. Meanwhile, Lt. Sheldon felt the sweat run down his face and his legs start to get heavy. Since we knew Jan was on the edge, we approached the mess hall very slowly not daring to remove our pistols since we also knew this would only upset Jan more.

Suddenly the door swung open and Jan stood with rifle in one hand and Lt Sheldon in the other. Shouting something in Polish, he then pushed Sheldon towards us and he fell over; we then assumed Jan was letting him go. So, I instantly ordered the men not to fire, just in time it seems because many of them had their fingers on the trigger.

Suddenly, in a fit of rage, Jan swung the rifle around and smashed it into pieces on the ground as he began to yell what we assumed were obscenities at all and sundry. Colonel Brown, meanwhile, had sent out for an interpreter and upon his arrival Jan seemed to calm down enough to be taken under guard towards the provost hut. It became clear that he thought he was being left behind to do all of the dirty work.

He swore he had no intention of hurting Lt. Sheldon and that he would have cut him down had matters got worse. Sheldon was rushed to the local hospital for a check-up since he felt he had been manhandled. Jan pleaded his innocence since he never understood what was happening but this fell on deaf ears, and he was placed under close arrest before being locked in a cell.

This was like locking up a caged animal since he reduced it to a heap of rubbish. For his own safety, and of course his jailers, he was shackled to the hospital bed. For what he did to Lt Sheldon alone would carry a long sentence, but for stealing a rifle and ammunition, I would assume put Jan away for a long time. I also felt for what he did regardless of the language problem he knew right from wrong, and for that, I felt Jan deserved some kind of punishment. Then again who knows - had he been told he was due to be shipped out maybe, just maybe, things would have been different. Was he another victim of circumstances or was he guilty as charged? We will never know if Jan had been treated fairly and given a better job how things might have worked out.

Although he was to remain under close arrest until the outcome of the trials, I made doubly sure each time a letter arrived from Poland addressed to him he got it straight away. His sister Krista wrote to him nearly every week since she was perhaps the one person in the world Jan could confide in. Krista knew her brother was just a gentle giant and would not hurt a fly unless he was put upon, so she knew he did not mean to hurt anyone during the fracas. Jan could possibly break a man's neck with one hand and cradle a mouse in the other. Krista knew her brother was capable of these things but also knew he must have been subjected to abuse on the day of his outburst.

****

Lt. Smithers found those facing a court martial had at least one thing going for them, and that was their bravery during action in the war. Lt. Smithers felt maybe this would affect the judge's decision when summing up. Lt. Sheldon wanted blood for the offences he had endured, and he was fast becoming unpopular with his fellow Canadians.

The trials began in earnest as thrice wounded Private Paul Riley stood accused of vandalism and looting government property, as he stood nervously waiting as Lt. Smithers once more stood to his feet and without blinking an eye said, "It would seem gentlemen that the accused Private Riley, a man with an exemplary record of bravery, acted out of character;

a man of Irish parents who immigrated to Canada in the hopes of a better future?"

Riley had, in fact, drunk so much on the day of the riot, and upon hearing the ships were not available had found himself intoxicated because he had a son in Canada he had never seen! He was sorry for his actions and blamed it on alcohol, but felt he and his fellow rioters had been treated unfair.

# Chapter 8

Lt. Smithers finished summing up and suddenly Riley was called to attention.

"It is the finding of this court martial you should be sentenced to one year in prison," the General, who was sitting in the middle with medals almost covering his chest, said, "If you don't have any drink for a while maybe you will return home a better person."

He continued as Riley sprang to attention and said, "Thank you, sir. I reckon I will behave myself since I dearly want to see my son," and he was led away.

One of the accused I felt no compassion for was private Valencia Mika, a Czech born infantryman who had said he enlisted because his mother and father were so poor they could not support him any longer. A short man in stature, Mika stood accused of inciting some one hundred men into rioting; he enlisted their help in releasing sixteen of his hardened friends from the guardroom, then smashing the canteen. Mika blamed his life of poverty for his sudden outbreak, but this fell on deaf ears since the panel was unimpressed by his constant pleading, and since he was a ringleader, they sentenced him to ten years penal servitude. His outbreak in the court room did nothing to make the panel change their minds.

The Liverpool Courier was the first to jump to his side by saying the sentence was too harsh, but Lt. Smithers said, "Someone had to be made a scapegoat."

Mika was to be an example to the others. He would be allowed to appeal at a later date they said.

****

I had begun to stop reliving the nightmares I had experienced when the war ended, that is until that evening on the train heading for Abergele. I felt myself dozing off as the rain began to fall on the train window. My tunic felt wet from the constant rain, and as I stared down at my boots, it was clear they offered little or no protection from the rain filled trench. The shelling resumed and the screams of men who were either wounded or were waiting to die also resumed. I sat down in what was now a half-filled trench and put my hands over my ears so as not to hear the screams, screams that will remain with me forever. As I sat trying to ignore what was going on all around me, I began to wonder why indeed we were trying to kill each other for what was in fact a piece of land.

Smoke bellowed through the open carriage window making me cough and at the same time bringing me back to reality. Closing the window, I glanced around the carriage hoping my return to the battlefield had not been noticed; luck was on my side since the carriage was empty. As the train continued its journey, I glanced out of the window only to be confronted by a picture of myself in battledress ready once more to command the men to go over the top and face the enemy. As I vanished through the smoke, I was suddenly confronted by five young men who appeared at the window, each one disappeared leaving me kneeling on the ground holding Private Henry in my arms with blood running down his face and him pleading with me to let him die.

The train's whistle brought me back to reality, the reality that the war was over and I was on my way home. Of course, I was concerned for Mildred and our forthcoming event, but that evening she knew something was wrong as she said, "George, you are not letting the court martial get to you, are you? You are not responsible for their actions."

"No, my love," I replied. "It's these damn dreams of mine. Each time I close my eyes, I see men dying in conditions you could never imagine; men, no boys, hardly old enough to drink let alone face the enemy."

Mildred placed her hand on her stomach and said, "I went to see Dr. Hughes today, and he said everything's fine. He was called to go up to the camp, seems they are sending the single men home first leaving the married ones until last. Of course, fighting began again and he was asked to tend the wounded since the camp doctor was amongst those wounded. I felt sorry for him since he is very old and fighting men is not what he needs at his age."

As we sat by the open fire Mildred said, "I happened to pass the church today and I noticed women dressed from head to toe in black. Nothing unusual you might say except she was kneeling and praying at the graves of those five men who were killed during the riot. As I stood watching her, she turned to face me, and I could see she had been crying. Suddenly, George, she rested her hands on one special gravestone, the gravestone of that Russian soldier, the one who died of a bayonet wound, er, Ivan Velitch, the vicar's wife told me. She was, in fact, the man's wife Maria Velitch. As she knelt, she uttered something which the vicar's wife said, 'She is asking us why her husband died in such a way. Perhaps only God knows the answer to that question.'"

After coffee Mildred continued with her fascinating story. "As I and the vicar's wife turned to leave, Mrs. Velitch said in broken English, 'You too have a husband buried here?' She glanced at my stomach and said, 'You have been left with child?' 'No,' I replied. 'My husband is an English officer up at the camp.' Well, George, I could not leave this woman on her own in a strange country, so I took her to the local tea shop."

Although it was now late, I felt I wanted to hear the rest of this story, so I said, "Please continue my love."

"OK, she told me she had saved enough to come to England by scrubbing floors and other menial jobs in what had become her home in Canada. Although Russia was her real home, she and Ivan had decided to live in Canada soon after getting married, she said. She wanted to start a family when the war ended but this was of course out of the question now. As she began to cry, I asked her where she was staying, and she replied, 'I have no place since I have spent all my money getting here.' George, I realize it was wrong of me and I should have asked you first but it's just until she can save enough to go back home."

"You mean," I replied, glancing towards our spare room.

"Yes, but please don't be angry with me," Mildred replied. "I agreed to let Maria stay on condition she helped around the house until the baby arrived."

Of course, Mildred was overjoyed at the prospect of a nanny. As we sat talking, I said, "I remember her husband well. The day he died his wounds were so bad nothing could be done to save him. He had been bayoneted in the stomach and bled to death, but how on earth did she get the money to come to England?"

Mildred replied, "From what I can gather she worked her fingers to the bone, and her only hope was to visit her husband's grave?"

# Chapter 9

Breakfast the following morning was to be a rather subdued affair not only because we now had a guest in the house but it was, in fact, the last day of the trials. The last man was to be sentenced.

We decided since she was tired from her journey and possibly had not seen a real bed for ages not to disturb her. As I placed my cap on my head I said, "I suppose you have realized my love we will have to tell our landlady of Maria and of how we hope she does not object?"

As the eight-fifteen pulled away, I reflected on Maria and of course Ivan. The picture of Ivan as the bayonet penetrated his flesh along with his screaming made me feel sick inside. The mental picture of Ivan with his hands covered in blood will perhaps rank alongside the one I have of Private Henry.

****

Lt. Sheldon felt he wanted revenge for his treatment at the camp and this became clear on the final days of the trials because he had made up his mind Private Alain Goff, an ex-machine gunner, was not going to get off that easily. Lt. Smithers and I were able to talk to Goff prior to him entering the court room, and he never once denied his actions, but it became evident he hated Sheldon mainly because at the hearings earlier Sheldon had stated Goff had aimed his rifle at a fellow officer and fired over his head. Asking him to produce the officer, he had a lapse of memory. It became clear Goff never held a weapon in his hands save for a handful of stones, and it seemed more and more of a lie since Sheldon was unable to produce the officer in question.

Sheldon, not to be outdone, decided to give evidence that Goff was one of the leaders. "This man," he stated, "was in my opinion one of the most dangerous of them all. He incited the men to riot and tore the British flag from its pole. He is, sir, a hardened troublemaker who I feel should receive a sentence to match his crimes and that should be one of hard labor."

Since it was obvious someone was lying, the panel of officers decided to delay sentencing Goff for one week to give Lt. Smithers time to find out the true facts. As this was announced, Lt. Sheldon stormed out of the courtroom with a look of disgust on his face. Lt. Smithers and I knew the man was lying just to get revenge on him being taken hostage and that he would not get away with it. As I entered the house in anticipation of meeting Maria, I wondered how Mildred had told our landlady of our visitor.

"George, I would like you to meet Maria Velitch. You, of course, knew her husband," Mildred said pointing towards a young girl only five-foot-tall with long black hair, not what I had thought Russian women looked like at all.

Maria could not speak hardly any English, but what she had command of she made the most of. "I am thinking, Mr. George, you and your wife are very kind."

I looked at her and replied, "I knew your husband, and he was a brave man."

Strange as it might seem, I wondered why a very poor Russian woman would work her fingers to the bone just to see the grave of her dead husband. Perhaps she wanted to prove to herself he was indeed dead, or she loved him so much she felt if she saw his grave it would be as though they were still together. She told us she came from a large family of six children and her parents were unable to feed and clothe them all. They would beg for food outside of restaurants until as a teenager she could stand it no longer.

Her father died of cancer four years earlier and her mother worked herself to death trying to bring up the family. She told us her brothers and sisters lived in the Ukraine and that she had not seen them for many years.

"Maybe it's time you returned home to your family you know Maria since you are alone in the world?" I replied as she fell asleep.

\*\*\*\*

Whilst the two women slept the next morning, I decided to join Lt. Smithers in his quest to find the truth. As I made my way towards the officer's quarters, I felt many of the men were still unhappy and not about to disclose any information that would help Private Goff. As we began to doubt whether we could save Goff from his fate, Smithers noticed a gang of men sitting around the base of a large oak tree.

The men laughed when Smithers and I saluted them and a stocky, shaven headed man put out his foot so that Smithers fell over it.

"Oh dear, sorry sir I never saw you." he said, as the men began to laugh.

Shaven head took charge as he said, "Private Williams, Sir, at your service, but you better hurry sir because we are on the next ship home?"

Williams had spent four years fighting, and rumor had it he had killed many of the enemy with his bare hands.

"Sir Goff was standing next to me during the riot and all he had was a handful of stones not a rifle in sight. Sheldon is nothing but a liar and is only seeking revenge for what Jan did to him."

Private John Williams was indeed an extrovert in many ways; his presence as he entered the public house was clearly noticeable, his size and his mean look told you he was not the man to spill your drink over. I had purchased three pints, and as he sat down and wrapped his large hand over his glass, I noticed the words H.A.T.E. tattooed on each finger.

Lt. Col. Lewellin, officer in charge of the Canadians and their repatriation, gave permission for Williams' statement to be written in his presence since the man was about to leave for Liverpool on his ship home. Sheldon was not to be informed of Williams's statement even though Smithers had gained evidence from the hospital that Goff was in at the time of the riot.

"Unfortunately, Private Goff would have been in no condition to do anything," the doctor said, "since he was unconscious."

He then gave Smithers a copy of Goff's medical file to produce in court.

The familiar sound of boots on concrete plus the noise from the other prisoners awoke Private Goff and a shiver ran down him as he glanced at the blanket on the floor of his cell. He swung his body off the bed, picked up the blanket, and wrapped it around his thin frame to ward off the cold.

"What the hell am I doing in here?" he said to himself. "Perhaps I should come clean and admit I shot myself in the barracks. After all, that bloody Sheldon will have me put away forever if I don't. I am a bloody innocent man, you hear me," he shouted as another voice replied, "We are all bloody innocent my boy, none of us did anything. I swear I never did that murder and old Jones in the next cell did not cut his wife's throat did you Jones? Anyway, he never meant to, did you?"

# Chapter 10

The exercise yard was perhaps the one place Alain Goff was able to collect his thoughts; thoughts of home and thoughts of friends he had come to make during his time in the trenches. He remembered one young man whose name he never had time to find out because as they shared a cigarette the young guy received a bullet through his head. Alain felt a twinge in his shoulder as the wound began to heal and his mind turned to thoughts of escape.

Alain then made the biggest mistake of his life. As he walked around the prison, he noticed the wall was seven or eight feet high, high enough perhaps for him to scale, but would he get shot in the attempt - this was his problem. At that juncture, Alain had no way of knowing Lt. Smithers and myself were gathering evidence to perhaps gain his freedom, or indeed that Williams had signed a sworn confession. Alain knew ships left every day since this was Liverpool and ships left all the time. He knew Sheldon was lying, and he also knew he would get away with his lies since he was an officer. Alain made up his mind he was going to join his pals onboard ship no matter what.

Alain had gotten used to seeing the guards have their usual smoke break. As they leaned their rifles against the wall and began talking, he slipped quietly over the wall unnoticed. Suddenly all hell broke loose as it became clear he had escaped. A bullet whistled past his ear as he ran for cover in the nearest building. He knew he had to make it to the docks no matter what!

"Bloody fool," the duty sergeant said, as he informed the duty officer, who was in a state of panic.

****

Alain felt the perspiration run down his back as his knees began to shake in fear. Suddenly in the distance, he heard the sound of a steamship, and he knew the docks were not far away and that meant freedom and a return home. Had he admitted to guilt by escaping he wondered as he ran towards the docks and the sea air became evident.

"Sheldon" he shouted. "Every dog has its day, and I will be waiting for you!"

As a whistle sounded and the sound of boots on concrete got nearer, he was confronted by one of the biggest ships he had ever seen as the SS Celtic stood in all her majesty in the light of the docks. With two armed guards on either side of the gangplank, Alain stood in the pouring rain five-hundred yards from freedom as one of the guards retorted. "Sod this mate let's call it a day. I have seen enough blood spilt to last a bloody lifetime?"

Alain hid behind a crate as the sound of footsteps increased and the rain began to penetrate his clothing. One of the last things he heard before the rifle hit him over the head was, "Here he is sir behind the large crate?"

**** 

Since the S.S. Celtic was about to depart the next day, many of the men from Kinmel camp had been transported to Walton Road Barracks in Liverpool. Of course, they were overjoyed at the prospect of returning home. Meanwhile Lt. Smithers and I were trying our hardest to get Sheldon to retract his evidence in time for Goff to maybe join his friends - of course we were completely unaware of Goff's daring escape bid.

It was during the time I was having tea with Mildred and Maria I received an urgent phone call to return to Kinmel camp immediately. Since I knew Mildred was now in safe hands, I quickly put on my uniform and made my way to the camp. It became clear to me that Alain Goff had indeed not escaped and was now in a prison hospital under heavy guard. I think, on reflection, I rather hoped he had made his escape and was on his way home! Lt. Sheldon had other ideas though and wanted him punished severely!

Alain Goff sat contemplating on how foolish he was since this time they were taking no chances by chaining his arm to the bed and putting an armed guard outside his door.

The metal cup hit the door as he shouted, "Does a guy get to use the John or wet the bed around here?"

The guard walked in with a bucket and said, "Take aim mate, you might even get it in the bucket?"

"But I want to…" Alain began, as the guy said, "Leave it to me. I will call a male nurse."

Since his health had improved Alain was moved back to prison. As Lt. Smithers and I awaited his appearance, we were startled to hear the sound of chains. As the door of the small room opened, Alain shuffled in with not only chains on his wrists but also on his ankles.

Lt. Smithers ordered the chains to be removed because, as he said, "He ain't about to go anywhere unless his name is Harry Houdini."

As the guard removed the chains from his wrists, he said, "Be it on your head, sir, he sure is a slippery one."

"I realize that, corporal, but running with your ankles chained is somewhat of a problem, agreed?"

As the handcuffs came off, Alain shook our hands warmly and said, "I know I have been a bloody fool, sir, but I could not face a prison term for something I never did."

His head was still in bandages and Alain Goff looked a broken man as he sat with his hands shaking.

"Could I please have a cigarette, sir?" he asked, and Lt, Smithers handed him the packet. As he lit his cigarette it was noticeable, he was either scared or had been beaten up, the latter it seems we would not be able to prove.

Lt. Smithers began, "It appears Alain you have more friends than you realize because we know Lt. Sheldon was lying, and you were, in fact, in the hospital the day of the riot. Private Williams, who I think you know well, has given us a sworn statement to this fact, but why did you not say you were in hospital, old chap? Plus, you have not done yourself any favors by escaping as you did. You know your pals are leaving in two days and that is precisely what we have to get you out of here. Never mind, old chap, I swear you will be on that ship if I have to put you on myself. Sheldon is not about to get away with this."

Lighting another cigarette Alain replied, "God bless you both."

\*\*\*\*

The Court Martial of Private Alain Goff on May 25th, 1919 was to be an informal affair since at the previous hearing his guilt had been proven, or so everybody thought save for Lt Smithers and myself. Alain was brought in dressed in a new uniform, his bandage removed and his hands in handcuffs.

As they led him towards the three colonels and two generals, I noticed a large swelling around his chin; leaning over to Smithers I said, "I say, old chap, those bastards have given him a going over, look at his chin."

Smithers answered, "George, they will only say he fell over. Let's get him free and on that bloody ship."

There was, of course, once again no mention of the five dead men, and the courtroom, filled with Press, seemed to say Alain was guilty as charged. Lt. Sheldon once more told his story which was complete fabrication and all that remained seemingly was his sentencing for, as they said, inciting a riot and aiming a rifle with intent to shoot an officer, plus escaping his Majesty's prison. Alain it seemed was heading for a long time behind bars - or was he?

Lt. Smithers, not to be outdone, jumped to his feet as it was seeming an open and shut case. Producing William's sworn statement, he then went on to produced evidence that Goff had not in fact used a rifle during the riot at Kinmel Army Camp.

Suddenly the courtroom became a slanging match as Lt. Sheldon stood up and shouted, "This trial is a travesty of justice."

That is when the presiding officers cleared the courtroom, saving for myself and Lt. Sheldon plus Lt. Smithers. Goff, meanwhile, was awaiting his fate in the dock as the judges replied. It would seem we should take in account your escape bid Mr. Goff, but time spent is prison is enough and we ask that you be returned home on the next available ship. As for you Lt. Sheldon, you are also to be returned home to

Canada, and we hope you have a safe journey?"

Alain Goff stood motionless as the verdict was read out, and he glanced towards Lt. Sheldon only the once!

The evening before the S.S. Celtic set sail for Canada the local public house rang with the sounds of joy, and after saying goodbye to Alain Goff, who would not stop thanking us, I turned to Lt. Smithers and said, "What of you now, my friend?"

"Well, George, after a well-earned rest perhaps I will return to Canada myself and look up that young nephew of mine. After all, I have got family I have never met. I believe he now has three children."

I shook his hand warmly and replied, "Well, if I am ever in Canada and I need a good lawyer I know who to call on."

As the nine-thirty train for Rhyl pulled out of the station, I felt a little sad the Court Martials were over, but overjoyed justice had prevailed and at the fact that I was soon to become a father. My only regret was five men died as a result of a riot that need not have happened. I, of course, had forgotten there were still men in the camp awaiting shipment home, and although I prayed peace had prevailed in the camp, I was entirely wrong.

# Chapter 11

Even before I arrived in Abergele, the newspapers were full of how Alain Goff was unjustly accused and of how Lt. Sheldon, an officer who had served with honor before going to Kinmel camp, lied to get revenge for being taken hostage, and still there was no mention of the five dead men.

As I placed the newspaper on the table, Maria said, "Why, sir, is there no mention of my Ivan in the paper?"

Unable to answer her question, I said to Mildred, "I sure am glad that's over and Sheldon got thrown out of the army."

As I glanced at Maria, she was sitting, head in hands, crying and speaking in Russian.

****

Upon my return to Kinmel camp, on the surface it was seeming things had returned to normality. The Lorries were being loaded and the men seemed overjoyed at the prospect of going home. The shopkeepers, knowing the money was also about to leave, had decided to close.

Visions of the riot came back to me as a gang of

men yelling obscenities tried in vain to turn one of the Lorries over. 'We were the first to go, them bastards jumped in front of us!' I thought to myself here we go again as the leader who did the shouting began once more to shake the lorry. I remember this man clearly since he was involved in the first riot but hid like a rat leaving the others to take the blame.

He was, in fact, an Indian by the name of Russell Yellow Hand, a man who had struck fear into many of those in Kinmel by his fearsome scream and his powerful build. As his massive frame began to turn the lorry over, it was noticeable he had streaks of paint on his face, and we deduced this was war paint.

One of the doors opened and out rushed a band of men carrying rifles: suddenly the sergeant of the guard, a well-built Scotsman, shouted "Fix bayonets, me lads."

The familiar sound of steel being inserted on the rifles echoed around the camp as Yellow Hand turned to face the guard who had by now completely surrounded him and he let out a wild, piercing scream.

I felt another death was in the air as the blade shone in the sunlight as Yellow Hand lunged towards Jock's stomach.

It was that moment I decided enough was enough by stepping forward saying, "If you drop the knife, we will make sure you are on the next ship home."

The sound of the rifle almost deafened me as Jock

pulled the trigger, saying, "He would have had you, sir, no trouble."

Yellow Hand was clutching the gaping hole in his stomach as the blood ran over his hands, and he fell to the floor shouting something in Indian which I figured was his last wish.

Suddenly Jock yelled out, "One of you go get the doc! I had to do it, sir, he was about to stick you with that knife."

"I know, Sergeant, but surely we have seen enough killing to last a lifetime?"

As I stopped talking, Private Yellow Hand yelled out something in Indian before dying. We were to find out later he was, in fact, an Indian chieftain, and his body would have to be returned to his tribe. Jock was, of course, admonished from blame since he was saving not only his life but my own.

Since the amount of publicity over the recent riot and the trials an immediate ban was put on the Press finding out about another death in the camp, but somehow news got out and once again, Abergele was on the front page. Yellow Hand's body lay in the chapel until his tribe in Canada sent for it. Yellow Hand did eventually get to his homeland, only it was to be in a coffin.

\*\*\*\*

Maria soon became homesick, and when her

husband's back pay came through, she decided she wanted to go home to Russia. Her English had improved, but when she heard of another death at the camp this was too much for her to take, and almost three weeks after the death of Yellow Hand, Maria said goodbye to her husband's grave and left for Russia.

As we said our goodbyes, Mildred began to get pains and that evening, she gave birth to a baby boy. Maria, of course, stayed a few more days to help Mildred, and we named our son John Henry Sawley, after the young man who died so bravely in my arms.

We eventually received a card from Maria saying she had remarried and guess what his name is? Yes, Ivan, and he had also served in France.

****

Perhaps you are wondering what happened to those remaining in jail. Well, almost all of those involved in the Kinmel camp riot of 1919 were released and were sent home to Canada by November of that same year, so perhaps the riot and those deaths were in fact all for nothing.

I received a letter in January 1920 from a Mr. Alain Goff, and it seems unemployment was still an issue in Canada, so he had decided to return to his homeland in South Africa to find his roots. We received one more letter from him saying a Mr. Sheldon was recognized by some of the men from Kinmel camp, and he received the beating of his life before fleeing to America. I seriously suspect Alain had something to do with Mr. Sheldon's sudden departure.

To end, he said something that will remain etched on my mind forever and it was, "We just wanted to be treated like men, we wanted more officers like yourself who cared about us. You can tie the rot down to lack of concern and in conditions unbearable. We had no compassion for our cause; with lousy officers like Sheldon what can you expect. I have the deepest respect for you and Lt. Smithers but had you been in the same conditions would you not have objected?" It was signed. "Ever grateful, your friend for life, Alain Goff."

Nobody was ever charged with the deaths of those five young men, and indeed, one would assume they were either killed by their own men or by advancing troops. Either way we must today assume their deaths were purely accidental.

I remained at Kinmel long enough to see the last of the Canadians leave, but strangely enough, it became clear there was to be a strange, bizarre twist to the story of the Kinmel camp riot of 1919.

As I opened my daily intake of mail, I noticed one of the letters had a Canadian Maple leaf on it. As I tried to think who could have sent it, I realized it was from Toronto General Hospital and read:

*Dear Sir,*

*I expect after all this time you are a little surprised to hear from me, but as I have only six months to live, I want to put the record straight. A grave injustice was done during the court martial. The court was wrong to let Private Goff go free since I lied about him being in hospital and forged the papers from the hospital. He was, in fact, in the camp and did fire over the head of that officer as Mr. Sheldon said. I understand Goff is known in South Africa? I only hope he can live with a lie because I fear I cannot leave this world knowing I lied to get him home with us. Please, sir, forgive me for lying to you and the court.*

*Sincerely yours,*

*Mr. Williams*

Justice did, in fact, prevail because Goff died robbing a bank in South Africa many years later. On his deathbed, he confessed to killing at least one of those in St. Margaret's and that was Private Ivan Velitch, Maria's husband.

The rain began to get heavy as did the burden of knowing I had helped free a guilty man, and as the French windows began to rattle, I glanced outside at the large puddle that has formed only to see the reflection of Private John Henry raising his arm in a farewell bid.

"George, you must have fallen asleep, your tea has gone cold," Mildred said, as she entered the study.

As the faces of those men came to me one by one reflected in the puddle, I lifted my arm to wave goodbye and said, "We will never forget you."

Mildred replied, "What did you say, George?"

"Nothing my love," I replied.

*A Time remembered of days gone by*

*A Time remembered to wonder why*

*A Time to ponder and maybe dream*

*A Time to wonder how life may have been*

*A Time to reflect on those we loved*

*A Time they may look down from above*

*A Time to maybe shout out loud*

*A Time to stand tall and proud.*

**The End, or Possibly…The Beginning!**

 **Author Robert James Bridge** began writing many years ago mainly because he has an imagination that tends to take him into a sort of dreamworld. At 82 years old, he still writes to this day, simply because he loves what he does; even if it pays very little.

Robert lives with his long-suffering wife, who has recently been given the all clear from cancer. He indicates she is long-suffering, because she has helped him to continue to write and given him the inspiration to carry on writing. Robert and his wife, Lilian, live on the South Coast of the United Kingdom, five minutes from the seaside.

Lightning Source UK Ltd.
Milton Keynes UK
UKHW020705051022
409964UK00019B/1493

9 781952 894367